Deckchairs

Five short plays

Jean McConnell

Samuel French — London
New York - Toronto - Hollywood

© 1995 BY JEAN MCCONNELL

Please see page iv for further copyright information

Edmund Price (signature)

DECKCHAIRS

Five short plays:

Shoppers
Early Blight
Dancers
Late Frost
Doggies

COPYRIGHT INFORMATION

(See also page ii)

AUTHOR'S NOTE

Each play is approximately fifteen minutes long and can be performed together as a group or individually.

Shoppers, *Dancers* and *Doggies* are comedies. *Early Blight* and *Late Frost* are dramas.

Deckchairs requires a cast of two women — the characters are different in each play. The scene — two deckchairs on a seaside promenade — is the same throughout. Beachchairs — e.g. "director's" chairs — may be used.

*Other plays by Jean McConnell
published by Samuel French Ltd:*

A Lovesome Thing

SHOPPERS

CHARACTERS

Rosemary
Angela

Scene — a seaside promenade
Time — the present

The promenade of a seaside resort. A sunny day

Two empty deckchairs are set C, facing front

Rosemary enters. She is a smart, middle-aged woman. She carries a handbag, pretty shopping bag, and several large carrier-bags from such stores as Debenhams, Bentalls, Dingles, M & S, etc. She looks about, consults her watch, then comes down and dumps her bags in one chair and sits in the other. She rubs her ankles and circles her feet, then repairs her make-up

Angela enters, looking about. Rosemary waves to her. Angela is also a well-dressed woman, and wears pretty ear-rings. She also carries a handbag, shopping bag and large carriers, one of them from W H Smith. Both women have well-to-do accents

Rosemary Coo-ee!
Angela Yoo-hoo!
Rosemary At last!
Angela Here you are!

Rosemary takes her packages off the chair and Angela flops into it, dumping her own bags beside her

Angela You've done rather well!
Rosemary Look who's talking!
Angela Debenhams? I didn't see you in there.
Rosemary I didn't stay more than a tick. I do think those assistants are getting a bit long in the tooth. There's one on the fancy goods ——
Angela I know who you mean!
Rosemary But I got the handbag I was after. Got two actually.
Angela Naughty!
Rosemary How did you get on?
Angela Three Susan Woolf blouses in Fangles.
Rosemary Angela! I thought you wanted a cashmere sweater?
Angela Didn't have them, my dear. Definitely going downmarket, don't you think?
Rosemary There were lovely cashmeres in Hoopers.
Angela Oh? Well, I can't go back. Not today anyway.

Rosemary No, not today.

They settle down

Angela Nice of Herbert to collect us.

Rosemary I said we'd be here on the front near the pier. He's at golf. Spends half his life there nowadays. Not that I mind.

Angela No. Clive's the same since he's retired. I hardly know the difference from when he was in the City. If anything he leaves the house earlier ...

Rosemary And comes back later!

They chuckle

Angela Nice for them to have a hobby.

Rosemary Everyone should have a hobby.

Angela I do so agree. We're lucky, I suppose.

Rosemary Yes. Bridge Mondays ...

Angela Health club Tuesdays ...

Rosemary Meals-on-wheels Wednesdays ...

Angela Oxfam Thursday ...

Rosemary
Angela } (*together*) And Fridays ... the shops!

Rosemary The weeks fly by.

Angela I like Fridays best.

Rosemary Definitely has the edge on meals-on-wheels.

They laugh

Angela I got a Janet Reger cami. (*She fumbles in a bag*)

Rosemary You never did!

Angela brings out a wisp of satin and lace

Angela Isn't it heaven?

Rosemary Is it for you?

Angela Why?

Rosemary Did you try it on?

Angela gives her a peeved look. She folds up the garment and puts it away

Rosemary (*placatingly*) You have such good taste.

Angela Mm. My mother always said good taste is an instinct. You've got it or you haven't. Like good manners really.

Rosemary Yes.

Angela Good manners are being aware of what might offend or upset the other person, my mother always said.

Rosemary Quite a pundit, your mother.

Angela A wise and cultivated woman.

Rosemary So it seems.

Angela Did you get anything special?

Rosemary I was mad for a little Robert Klein waistcoat I saw. But it really was quite out of my range. I went into Jones. It was quiet in the hosiery department so I took advantage of it. A dozen pairs of Dior tights.

Angela No! We must have just missed each other. I got six pairs myself.

Rosemary My dear, I thought the stand was a bit low on stock!

Angela Lower now!

They laugh

Rosemary Herbert always says I go through a store like a typhoon.

Angela Is Herbert still concerned about the market?

Rosemary You know Herbert — when prices are down he worries, when prices are up he worries. He's just a worrier.

Angela You know what my mother used to say about worrying?

Rosemary Worrying puts lines on your face?

Angela No.

Rosemary Don't worry it may never happen?

Angela No.

Rosemary I give up.

Angela My mother used to say about worrying — always let other people do it.

Rosemary Yes. I think you're right about your mother. She was pretty smart. Lived to a ripe old age no doubt?

Angela She's still alive.

Rosemary Oh. In a nursing home?

Angela No ...

Rosemary Sheltered housing?

Angela No. On a cruise.

Rosemary Ah.

Angela It was for her I got that beachwear last month.

Rosemary Oh? I did like those silk lounging pyjamas. Fancied those very much.

Angela Well they were from Debenhams. They may have some more.

Rosemary They did. But only on the model, unfortunately.

Angela (*rummaging in her bag*) Here, you have to see this darling little figurine. (*She produces a china statuette*) Royal Doulton!

Rosemary (*taking and examining it*) No, dear.
Angela It was on the Royal Doulton stand.
Rosemary I don't care. Look underneath.

Angela does so

Angela Good Lord, you're right! Well, how sneaky of them. It was definitely displayed on the fine china stand. There was the balloon woman and everything.
Rosemary It's quite pleasant.
Angela I'm half inclined to take it back. Try for a refund!

They laugh

Rosemary You do love a challenge, don't you, Angela. I thought I caught sight of you in M and S.
Angela I spotted you too.
Rosemary I did pop in for a quick browse.
Angela That's a contradiction in terms, Rosemary. You can't browse quickly.
Rosemary I'm sure I can.
Angela You rummage quickly. A browse is something you do slowly. Precise definitions make for clear communication.
Rosemary Your mother?
Angela Yes.
Rosemary She seems to have a pearl for every occasion.
Angela She does.
Rosemary I suppose we could do with some fresh ones. The old sayings don't seem to have an impact nowadays. Mind you, I've often wondered who made them up in the first place. Some are obvious, of course. "All work and no play makes Jack a dull boy" was obviously put about by Jack. But I don't understand half of them. I mean, "Many a mickle makes a muckle" — I ask you!
Angela It's Scots, Rosemary. It means if you save up enough mickles, then eventually it will turn into a muckle.
Rosemary Fair enough, I suppose. If you're into muckles.
Angela You haven't shown me in the big bag.
Rosemary Ah well, I do think I did rather well here.

She opens a large bag and brings out a woollen dressing-gown

Angela My!

Rosemary A hundred per cent Pyrénées. None of your "an Angora goat walked past it" rubbish.

Angela Beautifully warm.

Rosemary A nip in the air put it in my mind. Winter draws on!

Angela That reminds me. I picked up some thermal long-johns for Clive. We're going skiing at Christmas.

Rosemary Lucky you! Herbert will never hear of it. The nearest we get is the Wembley Ice Spectacular! By the way, how do you think those skating actors wish each other luck on the first night? They can hardly say "break a leg"!

They laugh

Angela (*thoughtfully*) Luck. It's a funny thing, luck. My mother always says ——

Rosemary (*interrupting*) Angela!

Angela Sorry. It's true. My mother does seem to have a profound observation to make on practically every topic.

Rosemary It's obviously a gift.

Angela It's a pain in the neck.

They laugh

Rosemary A lot of people would envy us our lifestyle, Angela.

Angela I don't know. There are plenty of women in our position. In the Home Counties anyway. And Wilmslow.

Rosemary Oh, I agree in the main. But they don't have that special stimulus that we have.

Angela On no. Not many get our sort of buzz out of life. But then, they wouldn't take our sort of chances.

Rosemary That's right. And if you take chances you need Fate on your side.

Angela And we have it!

They both sigh contentedly

Angela You're wearing a new lipstick.

Rosemary Picked it up this morning. Lancôme. There was a special display.

Angela It suits you. Not easy, lipsticks.

Rosemary Thanks. A very young girl on the counter. Usually the cosmetics assistants are over-keen.

Angela I know. Pouncing in with suggestions and advice. I'll never forget being literally forced to have a new make-up right there in the store. Wasted half an hour and finished up looking like Barbara Cartland.

Rosemary I managed to get some stickies for my false fingernails. Last lot had lost their glue. I found nine nails in my bed and one stuck to my shoulder. It gave me quite a turn.

Angela I imagine. Did you stop for lunch?

Rosemary No, just a break at eleven. Extraordinary thing happened. I bought myself a KitKat with my coffee and I got myself settled with all my gear and began my snack when I realized the man sitting opposite me was looking at me very strangely. Full of sort of — suppressed rage.

Angela Heavens! Did you move away?

Rosemary No. I out-faced him, glare for glare, as I drank my coffee and ate my KitKat. And at last he got up and went and bought himself another coffee and a bun and sat at a different table. But he kept staring over at me and when I left I gave him a very cold look, I tell you! And as I passed him he said the oddest thing. He said: "Would you like my bun?"

Angela What did you say?

Rosemary Nothing. I mean — definitely unhinged.

Angela Weird.

Rosemary You meet some odd people! (*She searches in her shopping bag*) I must show you the telephone jotter I found for Herbert's study. It's so unusual ... Oh!

Angela What's the matter?

Rosemary Oh dear.

Angela What? What?

Rosemary produces a KitKat from her shopping bag

Angela A KitKat?

Rosemary It must have dropped into my bag as I sat down at the table with all my packages.

Angela Rosemary!

Rosemary Oh heavens!

Angela No wonder he looked at you strangely — with suppressed rage — you were eating *his* KitKat!

They burst out laughing

Rosemary Fancy a KitKat?

Angela You are a case, Rosemary. (*She takes the KitKat and unwraps it*) Show me the jotter.

Rosemary searches in a carrier. She produces a belt, then another belt, then a jotter with a fancy cover. She shows it to Angela and stuffs the belts back

Rosemary There! See the price!

Angela My dear, it must be genuine leather.

Rosemary I should hope so.

Angela I'm sure Herbert will appreciate it.

Rosemary Oh, he's always delighted with my little surprise gifts.

Angela So's Clive. And he never asks to see the bill.

Rosemary Just as well!

Angela They know when they're well off. Not many men have wives as fulfilled as us.

Rosemary That's right.

They eat the KitKat between them

Angela It's nice they don't object to our Friday jaunts.

Rosemary Herbert says I do meals-on-wheels and Oxfam and the WI market so I deserve a little flutter on Fridays.

Angela Clive says the same.

Rosemary Let's face it, they do reap the benefit. (*She rises and crosses to throw away the KitKat wrapper*)

Angela Right. You haven't noticed my ear-rings.

Rosemary I did. Very pretty.

Angela Barbara Bosha Nelson.

Rosemary Oh! May I try them on?

Angela hands her the ear-rings and Rosemary puts them on. Angela holds up a mirror for Rosemary to see herself

Rosemary Gorgeous! (*Reluctantly she returns them*) I have my eye on something special in Laura Ashley's. But it will have to wait till next Friday.

Angela Laura Ashley's? Oh that's a lovely shop. And haven't they expanded? What are you after — a dress?

Rosemary No. A duvet.

Angela A what!

Rosemary A duvet.

Angela I'm not surprised you didn't get it this week — with everything else. But Rosemary — a *duvet*! You'll be setting your sights on a mattress next!

Rosemary I think I can manage it.

Angela Don't overstep the mark.

Rosemary But think of it ——

Angela You've got me worried.

Rosemary Oh maybe you're right.

Angela Do you need a new duvet?

Rosemary Oh no.

Angela Well then.

Rosemary I suppose I'm getting a teensy bit blasé.

Angela Now, Rosemary, that's fatal.

Rosemary I've just had things too easily. Been in the right place at the right time, you might say.

Angela Don't underrate yourself. Just think of that huge flagon of Madame Rochas you got last month. And you know it's your favourite. If that wasn't something! I've only ever seen that size as a dummy. I daren't even think of the cost.

Rosemary French perfume is grossly over-priced anyway.

Angela Oh Rosemary, you're a hoot. My sights are set rather lower. I mean to lay my hands on some Guerlain soaps next week. I love gorgeously smelly things in the bathroom. Did you go into the Ladies in Debenhams by any chance?

Rosemary No.

Angela A new air-freshener — quite lovely. Alpine breeze. (*She feels in her shopping bag*) I fell for it completely. (*She takes out a can of air-freshener and squirts it around*) Can't you smell the pine trees?

Rosemary We-ell ... I used the Powder Room in the Royal Hotel. They've completely refurbished it, did you know?

Angela Yes. I was in there last week. Quite charming.

Rosemary Must have spent a fortune on the fixtures and fittings. Those pretty hand basins and the fancy taps. And what about the little gold filigree mirrors?

Angela So sweet.

Rosemary And the matching hangers. Sort of art deco. Such an original design!

Angela Never seen any like them before.

Rosemary I just loved them. What's the time. (*She consults her watch*) Quarter to ... Angela, I think I'll just nip back there before Herbert comes.

Angela You think?

Rosemary Would you hold the fort here?

Angela Of course.

Rosemary rises. She picks up her shopping bag. She takes out a screwdriver. She flourishes it

Rosemary Good thing I brought this along.

Angela You're always so resourceful! Need a carrier?

Rosemary No, thanks. I have one.

Rosemary puts the screwdriver into her handbag, picks up her shopping bag and starts off

Rosemary I shouldn't be a tick — with a bit of luck!
Angela My mother says you make your own luck.
Rosemary She's so right. Be back soon!

Rosemary exits

Angela (*calling after her*) Don't worry, I've got the new best-seller from Shirley Conran!

Angela picks up a W H Smith carrier bag. From it she takes a map, a video cassette and a packet of envelopes. At last she brings out a Jackie Collins novel. She looks at the cover.

Oh no, it's the new best-seller from Jackie Collins. Even better!

Angela settles down to read as the Lights fade to Black-out

EARLY BLIGHT

CHARACTERS

June
Helen, her elderly mother

Scene — a seaside promenade
Time — the present

The promenade of a seaside resort. A sunny day

There are two deckchairs C, facing front. Helen, an elderly woman, is sitting in one of them. She has her legs wrapped in a rug, and she has a walking stick nearby. She peers about in an aggrieved manner. She takes her stick, attempts to rise but sinks back, wincing. She sighs crossly

Helen's daughter, June, enters. She is a middle-aged woman, attractive in a rather faded way. She is not hurrying. As she approaches the chairs, she pauses and looks down at her mother thoughtfully. June is carrying a bag of knitting. As soon as Helen spots her daughter she begins to speak in a complaining whine

Helen Ah! At last! Well, I must say you've taken your time. You stopped and had a cup of tea, I suppose. Well, give me my knitting then. That's what you were supposed to have gone back home for, wasn't it? Not to go off on some frolic or other and leave me sitting here twiddling my thumbs. You know I like to keep my fingers busy. They can be active even if my legs can't. Well, sit down, June, for goodness sake. Don't hover over me like some bird of prey!

June hands Helen the knitting bag and seats herself in the second deckchair. June looks out front, her face serious and thoughtful. Helen opens her knitting bag and sorts it out. During the ensuing dialogue she occasionally knits a stitch or two

It didn't occur to you to bring my reading glasses I suppose? Well, it doesn't matter since I'm on the plain stitch. Not that you knew that, did you? You're getting very forgetful, June, you know that? *I'm* supposed to be the old lady. Alice only said to me the other day, "Your daughter forgot to leave my money out, Mrs Hindle. Now *you* wouldn't have done that, Mrs Hindle. Razor-sharp, your memory". And she's right. You're getting thoroughly absent-minded, my girl, if even Alice has noticed it. I hope you remembered to put that casserole in. Don't want to sit here in the sun looking forward to a nice lunch and then find it not even started. (*She fumbles with some balls of wool*) This doesn't match, you know, June. I said it didn't. I did tell you the number. I suppose you forgot to write it down. Or lost it more likely. If only I could get out myself ... (*She sighs and glances at June*) I don't exactly run you off your feet, June. My needs are

reasonable, I'd say, for one in my position. We've a frugal way of life,
heaven knows. We don't exactly live on the fat of the land. Sometimes I
wonder why there's all this scrimping and saving. You've got my widow's
pension and now your state pension as well. What do we do with it all, I
ask myself. I'd like to see your bank account one day, my girl. I expect I'd
get a surprise. (*She laughs as if it's meant to be a joke*)

June does not react

I'm fed up with that hoki, I tell you. How long since we had a nice bit of
halibut? Eh? When I'm gone I expect it will be halibut halibut halibut.
(*Pause*) Some daughters talk to their mothers. Especially when they've
only got each other. Especially when one is virtually house-bound. A bit
of a chat wouldn't go amiss! (*Pause*) I'm knitting this for you, you know.

*Pause. At last June speaks although she still does not look at Helen. Her voice
is quietly anguished*

June Mother, why did you do it?
Helen (*puzzled*) What? What are you talking about?
June (*slowly and carefully*) When I went back to the house just now, I had
a little accident.
Helen An accident?
June I knocked something over. Broke something ... accidentally.
Helen Oh really, June. How clumsy. What have you broken, for heaven's
sake?
June I broke the blue vase.

*There is a terrible silence. Helen reacts first with shock then with great
discomfort*

The vase fell to the floor and shattered, Mother. And do you know what fell
out of it?
Helen No. No.
June I think you do, Mother.
Helen Blue vase ... blue vase ...?
June The blue vase that has stood on the stand in that dark corner of the
sitting-room for as long as I can remember. The blue vase with the Chinese
pattern, which you once said was rather valuable and was not to be handled
or moved unnecessarily. How many years has it stood there? Well, it's
lying on the floor now. And its contents, Mother, were a great surprise to
me. As you can imagine. (*Pause*) You don't seem to have anything to say
now, Mother. That is a surprise in itself.

Helen (*after a long pause*) June ...
June Yes, Mother?
Helen June ...
June Yes?
Helen (*deciding to brazen it out*) I can't think what you could have found in the vase.
June Then I'll tell you. Letters, Mother. Letters date-stamped *forty* years ago. And who do you think they were addressed to? Me, Mother. Seven of them in all. Seven unopened airmail letters.
Helen In the — blue vase, you say?
June Stuffed down into the blue vase, yes. Could have been there for all time. Is that what you hoped, Mother?
Helen June ...

June turns, and for the first time looks squarely at her mother

You led me to believe he never wrote.
Helen (*very uneasy now*) I ... I ...
June How did you manage to waylay the post? I looked for a letter. God knows, I looked for a letter. How did you manage it? But you were spry in those days, weren't you. Not like now. Did it happen easily the first time? You found it on the mat before me by chance? And it gave you the idea?
Helen It — it wasn't ever easy.
June Oh, I don't suppose it was later. You must have had to lurk and scheme and plot to get to the post before I saw them. *My* letters, Mother. If I'd ever had a suspicion you'd never have brought it off. But it never crossed my mind. Never.
Helen I did it for your own good.
June Oh, Mother ——
Helen He was wrong for you.
June Don't. Just don't.
Helen I had to take some action.
June So why didn't you destroy the letters while you were about it? Why did you just hide them away? Mm? I know. Because you knew in your heart it was a wicked thing you were doing. But you might just as well have torn them up and burnt them, destroyed them completely ... Because you certainly destroyed my life!
Helen I didn't mean to do that ——
June Oh really? What was it all about then? Don't say you didn't know what he meant to me. Seven letters he wrote, Mother. I have them here.

June takes the seven airmail letters out of her handbag. Helen eyes them fearfully

Helen I never opened them, June.

June Oh my! Should I say thank you for that? I've opened them, Mother. I've just opened them and I've just read them — forty years late. You know, if you *had* opened them and read them, Mother, you couldn't have kept them from me. Not even you.

Helen turns away from June

Look at me, Mother. Would you like to know what was in them?

Helen No ... no ...

June Well, I'm going to tell you just the same. Don't worry, I won't read you the loving parts.

Helen He didn't love you!

June Oh, Mother. He loved me more than I could ever have hoped for. He loved me and he sent for me. Here, see this first letter — full of hopes and plans for us. There is even money in it, Mother. Money for my fare to Australia. He kept his word. He sent for me. And I didn't reply. How could I? I didn't get the letter, did I? And he wrote again. And again. Here, see the letters — each more desperate and bewildered, Mother. The last one is so short and so hurt and so utterly despairing. Read it, Mother ...

June thrusts the letter at Helen

Helen No. I can't see. You know I can't see.

June You can see all right when it suits you!

Helen June, don't speak to your mother like that!

June I think you've lost any claim on me in that respect.

Helen (*spitefully*) So why didn't he ever telephone you? Have you thought about that?

June Didn't he? I wonder. I'll believe anything of you now.

Helen He did not telephone you.

June Perhaps not. He was no more self-confident than me. When I didn't write to him he must have thought it was just a passing fancy as far as I was concerned. Did you say anything to feed that thought before he left, Mother? Tell him I was very young and changeable by nature, for instance? Did you set some evil little seed like that? Did you? Did you?

Helen inclines her head, embarrassed. Then she becomes defensive again

Helen He couldn't have given you the sort of life you deserved.

June And that's what I've *had*, you think? Well, maybe you're right at that —

I should have followed my heart and somehow tracked him down. It must have been possible. Through Australia House perhaps. But no, I accepted that he'd gone back to his own country and taken up the threads of his old life and forgotten me. It was so terribly easy for me to believe it. You knew just the little hints and remarks to make, Mother. It was so terribly easy to accept that it had just been a temporary affair. That's how I came to see it — with your help, Mother.

Helen That's all it was! He was just using you!

June Don't tempt me to read you every word of these letters. He loved me — no question — and I broke his heart.

June hides her face in her hands in silent anguish. Helen watches her. She is shame-faced at last. When she speaks it is in an almost childish voice

Helen I didn't want you to go away, June. I didn't want to be left alone. I thought you'd meet some nice Englishman ... who'd take care of us both.

June Simple as that! Well, I didn't did I? I didn't want anyone else! There wasn't anyone else.

Helen That's nonsense, of course there was.

June If there was, I'd never have trusted them. My faith was wrecked for good, don't you see? Oh, but you do.

Helen I didn't intend that.

June No? It was just a convenient outcome, eh? I was all yours for ever afterwards. There wasn't anything better I wanted to do with my life. So you had a permanent companion — and later on a cook, housekeeper, hand-maiden — the lot.

Helen I know you've been a good daughter to me.

June I've been a bloody idiot.

Helen No, no! Don't talk like that. You're not yourself. That's not my Juney.

June Oh, shut up!

June puts the letters into her handbag. She handles them with great tenderness

Helen (*watching anxiously*) What ... what are you going to do?

June I'm considering. I think you've had as much of me as you've any right to expect in the circumstances, don't you?

Helen But June, I need you more than ever now. I can't walk without help. I can't manage in the house on my own, you know I can't.

June That's true. Nevertheless ——

Helen You're not thinking of trying to trace him — after all these years?

June I hadn't. But it's an idea.

Helen He's probably married — with a family — you'd make a fool of yourself.

June (*with a wry laugh*) It won't wash, Mother. I don't give a damn for anything you say any more. Making a fool of myself is what I seem to have done already ... for years and years and years. A real joke of myself!

Helen What will you do? You're not just going to move out of the house and leave me.

June No. I'm going to get out of this chair and *walk off* and leave you.

Helen You can't leave me here in a deckchair on the front!

June I don't see why not. Call out to a passer-by. Someone will stop eventually.

Helen Suppose they don't? I can't walk by myself!

June So you can't. You'll need a taxi. I'll call you one when I get home.

Helen Home?

June Yes. I'll go and pack my things. And then I'll ring a taxi and tell them where you are. They can send one to take me and one to fetch you.

Helen June! I feel ill.

June So do I, Mother. I feel a great pain inside me. A pain made up of sorrow and disillusionment and rage and bitter, bitter regret. It's a worse pain than arthritis, Mother.

Helen I think I'm going to faint.

June Then I'd better be off before you do.

Helen (*regaining some spirit*) You're hard-hearted! I never thought it of you. You know I only wanted what was best for you. You were well-educated, cultured ... you'd have been miserable on some sheep-station in the wilds of nowhere. You're romanticizing it all now. It was different at the time. I saved you from a hard, soul-destroying life.

June Mother, no life could have been as soul-destroying as mine with you. I didn't see it before. But now it's clear as clear.

Helen Where will you go? You've no money.

June I thought you believed I had. What about this nest-egg I've been saving out of the housekeeping? Perhaps I *have* got it after all. Thousands and thousands of pounds stashed away. I think I'll settle in the Bahamas.

Helen Now I know you're joking.

June You think I have a joke left in me right now, Mother?

Helen You'll get over this upset, dear. I don't think you realize what you've been saying. Go off on your own! I think you'd soon see you need me too.

June Oh? What for?

Helen Company for one thing. Who else have you got?

June I'm going, Mother.

Helen Go on then. You may walk to the end of the esplanade but that's as far as you'll get. You're not a young girl now, June. There's no turning back the clock.

June I'm going, Mother. (*She rises and picks up the walking-stick*)

Helen You're set in your ways, June. More than me, I'd say. You've got a good home and you can do things when and how you like ——

June Here's your stick, Mother. (*She places the stick on the back of her mother's chair*)

Helen You won't like it out in the cold, hard world, take my word. You won't find another job at your age if that's your idea. And you don't think your friends will take you in, do you? You haven't any worth speaking of any more, have you?

June And why's that?

Helen A hotel will be expensive. Do you imagine you'll get a flat? And sit all by yourself by a gas fire night after night? Lonely? Lonely?

June No, that's you, Mother. Not me. I've been alone inside for years. I'll find no difference.

Helen June!

June Goodbye, Mother. (*She starts off*)

Helen (*desperately*) June!

June pauses, then without looking back she straightens her shoulders and exits

Helen (*calling after June, confidently*) You'll be back! I'll give you to the end of the esplanade!

Helen sits upright. She knits a few stitches, defiantly. She looks off in the direction of June. Watching and waiting. She waits. And waits. She begins breathing hard. Her hand goes to her chest as a pain begins ...

The Lights fade slowly. Black-out

DANCERS

CHARACTERS

Wynn
Betty

Scene — a seaside promenade
Time — the present

The promenade of a seaside resort. A sunny day

Two deckchairs are set c, facing front. Wynn enters. Betty follows her. Both women are dressed-up for tea-dancing, and carry handbags and shoebags. Betty's frock is rather low-cut

Betty Oh Wynn, not so fast! Let's have five minutes!
Wynn You're on. What's the rush? Nice here in the sun.

Betty sits in one of the chairs. Wynn moves the other nearer to her

Betty Watch yourself with that chair, Wynn!
Wynn Don't tell me! Remember Colin?
Betty Poor Colin. These folding chairs are all very well, but I always remember Colin.
Wynn Poor old Colin.
Betty Still, he had it sewn back on.
Wynn Lucky for him.
Betty Yes. He was a lovely dancer, Colin.
Wynn I should say. Medallist you know.
Betty Not surprised. Pity he moved away. He'd have enjoyed these tea-dances on the pier.
Wynn Still he'd have brought his wife, no doubt.
Betty Yes.
Wynn Yes. Two left feet if not more.
Betty (*giggling*) Wynn! Wonder where they first met?
Wynn Well, it wasn't a dance!
Betty No! It was awful watching him yanking her round the floor. He was loyal, I'll give him that. Always gave her a good whirl.
Wynn Yes. They had six children.
Betty Wynn!
Wynn He looked marvellous with a good partner.
Betty I danced with him a lot.
Wynn So did I.

A pause

Betty Well, he's gone now. One less man.

Wynn There are the two new widowers — what are they called? Bill and
      Wally.

Betty Bill and *Morrie*.

Wynn Morrie?

Betty Morrie. Short for Maurice.

Wynn Oh. You soon found out.

Betty I danced with one of them.

Wynn Lucky you. They seemed to be hanging together a lot.

Betty Shy first time.

Wynn Didn't seem shy — laughing away in the corner.

Betty They're old friends.

Wynn Obviously. I thought they were going to dance together at one
      point.

Betty And why not, pray? Peggy and Elsie often do.

Wynn That's different. They'd look funny.

Betty So do Peggy and Elsie.

Wynn All right. You win.

Betty They'll soon fit in. I think I made Bill loosen up.

Wynn Well, if anyone could ...

Betty (*giving her a look*) I'll take that as a compliment.

Wynn I was sure someone said *Wally*.

Betty Look, he must know his own name!

Wynn I suppose so. They do sound alike.

Betty Wynn!

Wynn All right, all right. I broke the strap off my silver shoe. (*She takes a
      shoe out of her shoebag and examines it*) Luckily I could dance in these.
      (*She waggles her feet*) That *paso doble* takes it out of you. I'm sure it was
      faster this week.

Betty I think you're right. I was flying round the floor with Edgar.

Wynn I saw you.

Betty He has wonderful control.

Wynn Oh he has. There were others who gave up.

Betty Peggy and Elsie fell over.

Wynn It really was too fast.

They nod their heads. Then they begin to chuckle

Betty Did you see?

Wynn Who didn't! I thought those went out with the Ark.

Betty Bill and Morrie were helpless.

Wynn Yes, well, we'll get *them* going next week.

Betty We will.

Wynn Who said they were widowers?

Betty Ethel Prendergast.

Wynn Trust her to ferret it out. They seemed a bit merry for widowers. I thought they were probably divorced.

Betty I wonder.

Wynn Well you danced with one of them.

Betty Morrie, yes.

Wynn Could be happily married ... and needing a break from it.

Betty You are a cynic, Wynn.

Wynn I'm not, I'm C of E.

Betty gives her a push

Wynn I saw you dancing with that Stan Barnfather.

Betty I couldn't get out of it.

Wynn I know. These old-fashioned Paul Joneses are all very well but——

Betty Didn't enjoy it! I could feel his — you know — every time we did a dip.

Wynn His what?

Betty Oh God, Wynn ...

Wynn Oh! Gracious! He seems such a keen dancer.

Betty Well, he certainly wasn't concentrating on his feet.

Wynn They used to try that in the tango ... when we did the tango.

Betty Right. Now they go for the slow groove and a handful of buttock.

Wynn It's not dancing.

Betty Definitely.

Wynn But you are a very sexy woman, Betty.

Betty (*not displeased*) Am I?

Wynn You exude it.

Betty Do I?

Wynn So you can't blame him.

Betty Hold on ——

Wynn You see men aren't actually entirely in control of their urges. It's like there's a separate person they carry around in their pocket. You've surely seen that little book ...

Betty Little book?

Wynn This little person sees a woman he fancies and he perks up and says, "Go for it, Fred" — or whatever the man's name is. And maybe Fred says "Down Rover, that's the boss's wife". But Rover just goes on pressing the point — if you follow me. And giving Fred all sorts of excuses why it's OK to follow his nose.

Betty You do have a way of putting things, Wynn.

Wynn Well, it's a fact. If you don't want to arouse a man you don't go around giving off mating signals. Now take your cleavage ...

Betty I can't help having a cleavage. Either you've got a cleavage or you haven't. It's not something you can deflate.

Wynn Possibly ...

Betty What do you mean "possibly"!

Wynn But you don't have to put a frill round it.

Betty Anybody would think I was wearing a mini-skirt and a see-through blouse!

Wynn All I'm saying is, men can't always help themselves. If you're not selling fish don't lay out your slab.

Betty At least some of us have still got a salmon steak on offer. Not dried up old kippers like some people.

Wynn I think you're going a bit far!

Betty You started it!

Wynn I was merely commenting on the big difference between men and women. It's one of life's imponderables. Like when you pick up your tights in the morning and one foot faces in and the other out.

Pause

Betty Anyway, men lay out their wares as well. I had one boyfriend who wore half a tennis ball in his pants.

Wynn What?!

Betty Looked very virile until he took his trousers down. Then it fell out on the floor. And the cat started playing with it.

Wynn looks aghast

   With the *tennis ball*. Honestly, Wynn!

Wynn Oh Betty, really ...

Betty Cross my heart.

Wynn I've obviously moved in different circles.

Betty Very likely.

There is a cool pause

Betty Like a toffee? (*She produces a bag*)

Wynn (*taking one*) Thanks.

Betty Bill and Morrie seem like gentlemen. I wouldn't mind having a man about the place again. So long as he could mend fuses and all that. They can't always.

Wynn I can mend my own fuses.

Betty I'd have guessed.

Wynn What's that supposed to mean?

Betty Just, you're the capable type. I'm surprised dancing's your hobby. I'd have put you down for wine-making or car-maintenance.

Wynn I'm a silver medallist.

Betty You said.

Wynn I'd like to get my gold. Only I need the right man.

Betty With the right man everything would be gold.

Wynn If you believe that, you'll believe anything.

Betty He's out there somewhere.

Wynn Betty you've had your share. What happened to Julian?

Betty Julian? Ah, Julian. He took me out to dinner. And to the theatre. He spent weekends with me. He took me on a day-trip to France!

Wynn Someone said he dumped you for Alice.

Betty He did that too.

Wynn Now *that's* a dangerous lady.

Betty Right. It's always the quiet, faded, self-effacing ones, wearing sober clothes and the necklace their late husband gave them ——

Wynn And who can't reach the bookshelf. Are scared of mice ... enjoy ironing shirts ... make pies ... won't go out at night on their own ——

Betty They're the ones!

Wynn That's when you need to watch your back!

Betty Never give up until the ring's on their finger.

Wynn Snaffle a man from right under your nose.

Betty And right under *his* nose — without him having the least suspicion.

Pause

Betty } (*together*) Clever devils!
Wynn }

Wynn I'll settle for a dancer. He doesn't have to have anything else to offer. Not marriage or money or looks, or even a sweet nature ... Just so long as he has twinkling toes.

Betty Bill and Morrie aren't bad ...

Wynn Oh, we can do better than that.

Betty Yes.

Wynn Funny how few men of our generation are really good dancers. I've got this notion I'll make a life-size stuffed partner, and fix its feet to mine. That way we'd move as one, no problem.

Betty Even easier, you could buy one of those big blow-up dolls ...

Wynn What blow-up dolls?

Betty You know, the ones they sell in those shops ...

Wynn What shops?

Betty Forget it, Wynn.

Wynn What we could do with are some professional dance partners. With all the men out of work you'd think they'd have seen the opening.

Betty We ought to start an agency, Wynn. Escorts for widows.

Wynn Just for dancing, or squiring us to the theatre or to restaurants. You know ... nothing else.

Betty Oh no. (*Thinking again*) Well ... that would be up to the widow. I mean we could call the agency *Widows' Might*.

Wynn I was being serious, Betty.

Betty Me too.

Wynn We could call it *Gentlemen Friends*.

Betty I bet I know who'd be our first customers ...

Wynn Yes ... Peggy and Elsie!

They laugh heartily

Betty I've thought of another service they could give. They could go on holiday with us.

Wynn Oh no.

Betty Carry the luggage ... handle the tickets ... give us some clout with the hotel manager for a change!

Wynn Oh no.

Betty Why "oh no"?

Wynn Well you're surely not suggesting you share a double room?

Betty Oh no. Mm, not necessarily. No, definitely not.

Wynn There you are then, we're still stuck with the single rooms. And we've learnt about single rooms, I should think.

Betty You've got a point there.

Wynn With half the world living singly you'd think someone would get the message. I mean unless it's your spouse ...

Betty Or your lover ...

Wynn Who wants to sleep in the same room as someone else?

Betty It's my belief they enjoy watching perfectly good friends going off each other.

Wynn Yes. (*Pause*) Well, you know, Betty, I just *have* to sleep with the curtains closed.

Betty So I discovered. Like being buried alive.

Wynn You snore.

Betty Harry never complained.

Wynn Husbands get used to these things. You also call out "Peter" in your sleep.

Betty Peter? Ah. Yes, well — I'll have to watch that.

Wynn Be nice to go to the Lakes sometimes, together. But no double room.

Betty No. And no gigantic supplement for two broom cupboards!

Wynn No! So ...

Betty What about tents? One each.

Wynn Are you mad?

Betty (*sighing*) Be an activity holiday again then. Student rooms.

Wynn Fair enough. What do you fancy?

Betty Ballroom dancing?

Wynn What else. Maybe we could mention it to Bill and Morrie.

Betty No. Let's wait and see what's on offer at this year's course.

Wynn All right for you.

Betty Well ... Anyway, you had the Instructor.

Wynn Yes. He did choose to demonstrate with me. They need someone quick on the uptake.

Betty Pity that blonde took over mid-week.

Wynn I think he already knew her.

Betty If not he soon did!

Wynn (*after a sigh*) Ever thought of Folk Dancing? You don't need partners so much. Lots of hanging round the shoulders and whizzing in circles.

Betty Really?

Wynn Still, pretty exhausting.

Betty I prefer partners. It's more natural.

Wynn Agreed.

Betty Yes.

Wynn Yes.

They sigh. Wynn lies back in the chair, eyes closed. Betty reaches for her handbag and spots something off R

Betty Wynn.

Wynn What?

Betty Wynn!

Wynn What is it?

Betty It's Bill and Morrie.

Wynn (*sitting up*) Where?
Betty Just coming off the pier. Look.
Wynn (*looking off* R) So it is. Do you think they're headed this way?
Betty Don't know. (*Dismissively*) Who cares.
Wynn (*the same*) Quite.

Betty opens her bag, puts away her spectacles and primps in her mirror

   I can't see them for that kiosk. Maybe they went off to the town. No, there
   they are — coming this way.
Betty (*peering*) Yes. Oh! They're waving.
Wynn So they are. (*She fixes her hair and crosses her legs*)
Betty (*waving towards them, off* R) Yoo-hoo!
Wynn Betty, don't overdo it. (*Waving to them, off* R) Yoo-hoo!
Betty They're still waving.

Gradually the women stop waving

   Wynn.
Wynn Yes?
Betty I don't think it's us they're waving to.
Wynn No, I don't think it is.
Betty Then who ...?

The women swing across and look off L

Wynn My God, guess who!
Betty (*peering*) Who? Who?
Wynn Put your specs on, Betty.
Betty Wynn, you don't mean ——
Wynn I *do* mean. Waiting in that shelter. Peggy and Elsie!

The two women swing back, looking R. *Their eyes follow "Bill and Morrie"
as they approach and appear to pass in front of them. When the "men" are
level the women give them a limp wave, then go on watching as the "men"
exit* L. *Simultaneously, the two women slump back in their chairs*

Wynn Shit.
Betty (*with a sigh*) Agreed.

Betty and Wynn sit facing front for a moment busy with their thoughts

Then they rise, collect their belongings and with a toss of the head, stalk off

The Lights fade to Black-out

LATE FROST

CHARACTERS

Pamela
Kate

Scene — a seaside promenade
Time — the present

The promenade of a seaside resort. A sunny day

Two deckchairs are set C, *facing front. The murmur of waves is heard. Pamela and Kate are lying back in the deckchairs, basking in the sun. They both wear sunglasses and light clothes, suitable for a day by the sea. Both are middle-aged, smart, attractive women. There is a long pause before Pamela speaks*

Pamela Kate ...

Kate (*not moving*) Relax, Pamela. We've come down to the sea to get some ozone in our lungs and a kiss of sun on our faces. Relax.

Pamela But Kate ——

Kate Not a word, you hear me? Let it all flow over you. You need it. It'll help. Honestly.

Pamela But ——

Kate Pam, just lie back and enjoy it. It will do you good.

Pamela All right. (*She settles back*) This was a good idea.

Kate I told you so.

Pamela Yes. Thanks, Kate. You know ——

Kate You're not supposed to talk.

Pamela (*taking off her glasses*) I'm not going to talk about Robin. That doesn't mean ——

Kate I understand. (*Taking off her glasses*) Listen, you don't have to feel guilty for letting some other thoughts come into your mind besides Robin. It doesn't mean you care less or miss him less. It means you're starting to get on with life. So. I'll let you talk.

Pamela (*awkwardly but with feeling*) I wanted to say to you ... to let you know, somehow, how much I appreciate ——

Kate Oh my dear, now shut up, do. What are friends for, for goodness sake.

Pamela Well ... I've come to see that friends are for lots of different things. For having a laugh with. For ringing up when you're blue. For sharing good news with. For standing in when you need a baby-sitter, a dog-sitter, a mother-sitter ...

Kate Hold your horses, what's with this sitting business? I've never done any of that for you. Nor you for me for that matter.

Pamela Well, you would have.

Kate I'm not sure. Would *you* have?

Pamela In an emergency.

Kate You and your emergencies! (*She is trying to keep the conversation light*)

Pamela It's not the emergencies of life, of course. Everyone rallies round then. It's the day to day things. Those are what you need friends for. A friend is one who listens to you when you bad-mouth your mother-in-law and then forgets what you said. So you don't feel rotten when you're friends again with the old bat.

Kate I guess a real friend needs a good memory for shared joys and a bad memory for old scores.

Pamela I guess. (*Pause*) It's good knowing each other for such a long time, Kate. Means neither of us has to pretend about anything. You know where I come from. And I know where you come from.

Kate Right. I know what we made of ourselves after that pitiful education we had. What a school!

Pamela It wasn't all bad.

Kate Well ... No school that turns out two ignoramuses who still get good jobs and marry well-heeled husbands can be all bad. Hard luck they didn't stick.

Pamela Yes. But I had a second chance. I'm sorry you haven't found someone else. I know I was very lucky finding Robin.

Kate Pam ——

Pamela No, I want to talk about him just normally. I can now. It's waning, thank God, the emotion. So let me.

Kate (*after a small pause*) If you want to.

Pamela You're the only one who knows truly what he meant to me. Just as you were the only one who understood what I felt when the baby died. My little golden child ...

Kate Pam, it's a long time ago.

Pamela I know. But you were the only one I could have leant on like I did. It's not just knowing you are strong. It's knowing you cared for me honestly — wanted to bear it with me — it's the same now with Robin. I know I can talk of him to you because you loved him just as you love me. I was so lucky having him for all those years. (*Pause*) You know, Kate, you shouldn't have stayed so long in your marriage.

Kate Maybe. But it seemed right to go on trying. He seemed to need me.

Pamela All it meant in the end was that you were facing a new life so many years older.

Kate I wasn't so crazy to find another husband. I'd had enough of the married state, quite honestly.

Pamela But you needed a man, I know that.

Kate Yes, I needed a man. I wanted a man. But not there every day conditioning every move I made.

Pamela I know you believed your best intentions had been pointless, I know how undervalued you felt in the end.

Kate That's true. Time wasted.

Pamela Well, I just hope you've had plenty of the sweet things since. You deserve them, in my book.

Kate I've had my share of happiness, Pam. Plenty. I've been lucky too and that's a fact.

Pamela Still I wish you'd found a good husband, instead of ...

Kate Instead of what?

Pamela Oh Kate, I know how much your lover has meant to you. But it's not the same.

Kate You mean we must love each other less?

Pamela It has to be different surely. The way things are.

Kate We didn't come down here to talk in this way, Pam. We came down to enjoy the seaside, remember?

Pamela You have so much to give, Kate. I wanted you so much to find someone to make your life complete. As Robin did mine.

Kate Well, you certainly trotted out enough candidates!

They both laugh

Kate Remember Oliver?

Pamela Oh dear. He did seem a possible. Nice-looking, a good job. Charming.

Kate He was. He was. I hated him on sight. And he me!

Pamela I did my best.

Kate You were marvellous. I'd just become too choosy. Just wearing trousers is not enough recommendation.

Pamela Unlike Edna.

They both laugh

Goes through them like a box of chocolates.

Kate I should think Dateline see her as their pension.

Pamela She has her fun. And I know you enjoy your relationship, Kate. I must say you've been discretion itself. He must be thankful for that. I've guessed it has to be someone in public life. But I know I mustn't probe. I've accepted that.

Kate Can we leave it, Pam?

Pamela Yes, all right. I just feel that if you love each other so much, then he might have wanted to make his life with you. All right, you've said, he loves his wife too. But I don't see how he can.

Kate He wouldn't hurt her.

Pamela But don't you feel, just occasionally, that you've sacrificed too much for him?

Kate I might have thought that if I'd been younger. That's where it's different. I have a separate life of my own, a busy, satisfying life. But giving and receiving love needed to be a part of it.

Pamela Mostly giving it seems to me.

Kate Not at all.

Pamela I know I'll never marry again. I've had the best and dearest man in the world. No-one could ever take his place. I adored him, my darling Robin. He was — such fun!

Kate I know. And he loved you very deeply.

Pamela I couldn't have got through all this without you, Kate.

They smiled at each other fondly. Pamela leans forward thoughtfully. Kate leans back, busy with her own thoughts

He always wanted to be everywhere at once. He only chartered that plane so that he could fix some business in Glasgow and still keep appointments in London. Everyone expected so much of him.

Kate That's the way it is with giving people. Everybody wants more and more of them.

Pamela He was on so many committees, so many organizations. He had a way of making people get along together and achieve things.

Kate Yes, he did. They all respected him, valued his opinion, his judgement.

Pamela He was always off somewhere. They had him floating round the world, giving advice, supporting causes. I used to kid him he had a bimbo in every city.

Kate I don't think Robin was a man for one-night stands.

Pamela I wasn't serious. That wasn't his style ... casual sex.

Kate No.

Pamela No, it didn't matter where he'd been he would make it back to me. Sometimes, I longed to make love, but I could see he was tired. I would just hold him. We didn't have to pretend. But mostly it led to sex — passionate and sweet sex. All our life together, it was good. (*Pause*) All those people at the funeral. So many came up and said he had been their best friend — the kindest man they'd ever known. Many of them I'd never even met.

Kate He tried to please everyone. They all wanted their very own piece of him. Maybe it was all too much.

Pamela I don't think so. He wanted to live that way. It was part of his nature.

Kate Yes, you're right, of course.

Pamela You remind me of him sometimes, Kate.

Kate I do?

Pamela You're good fun and you're a caring person too.

Kate I don't know about that. I just know Robin was a very special sort of man. So full of life.

Pamela Oh yes!

Sudden pain crosses their faces

They said it had to have been instantaneous.

Kate We have to believe that, Pam. (*She turns away*)

Pamela When the news came I couldn't believe it. I'd heard on the radio — a light aircraft — crashed in a field. I'd no idea ...

Kate Pam ... (*She holds out her hand*)

Pamela (*taking it*) I tried to ring you at home. But you weren't there. You were the first person I rang. I needed you, Kate.

Kate I came as soon as I could.

Pamela I rang your office. They said you'd gone away for a couple of days. Up north. They wouldn't give me the number. I did try to contact you, Kate. You know that. I left a message. I knew it would be such a shock. But I had to let you know ...

Kate I came as soon as I could, Pam.

Pamela I didn't want you to hear it from anyone else. I explained to your secretary and she searched everywhere for a note of where you'd gone. At one point she said she'd found the number and she gave me the code, then she said the rest of it was illegible. I told her who I was and what had happened and then she said she thought you'd gone to Liverpool. I said that was the wrong code for Liverpool. It was really terrible. Is she usually so silly?

Kate No.

Pamela I couldn't get any sense out of her. I just had to track you down. But I knew she'd got it wrong because the code she'd given me was the code for Glasgow. O-one-four-one. Not o-one-five-one.

Kate is very still

And I knew it was the code for Glasgow because there it was staring me in the face on my telephone pad. Robin's hotel number in Glasgow. That code. I thought I'd go mad, Kate, sitting there in the house alone, desperately trying to get hold of you. You can't imagine what it was like. Oh I know you must spend a lot of time alone in your house. But you do so much travelling with your business, don't you? You're always away so much. Or used to be, didn't you? It's been sweet of you to keep me company so much these last months. I hope your work hasn't suffered.

Kate No. It's flexible. It always has been. And there hasn't been a need for me to go away so often lately.

Pamela I appreciate it.

Pamela is still holding Kate's hand in hers. A pause

It was such a relief when you finally came back and rang me. They all kept on at me to do this and do that. See solicitors. Make arrangements. Say how I wanted things done. I couldn't handle any of it. I told them all to wait until I'd talked to you. They asked if I didn't have any relatives. I said no-one who was like you. Kate is my lifelong friend, I told them. She'll understand. She'll help me. At last they all shut up.

Kate (*bleakly*) I came as soon as I could.

Pamela I think one way and another we scoured every likely inch of Liverpool. Guest houses ... hotels ... B and Bs ... (*she tails off*)

A very long pause, during which a thought slowly enters Pamela's head. She turns and looks fully in Kate's face, aware for the first time of her anguish

(*At last*) You weren't in Liverpool, were you?

Kate doesn't answer. Pamela removes her hand. Kate looks away

You weren't in Liverpool. You were in Glasgow. (*A pause*) Are you going to answer? (*A pause*) I suppose you have.

Kate Pam ——

Pamela No, stop! You have to let me get used to this. To arrive at something like this so suddenly ... so unexpectedly. It's sort of ridiculous.

Kate Yes, I agree. So many years when it mattered. And now when it doesn't ...

Pamela Oh, it matters, Kate! Oh, it matters all right! It changes everything. I don't think I can take this change. Robin! I feel as if I've lost him all over again. And this time completely.

Kate No, no, no! He was yours. Always was and always will be.

Pamela How could he!

Kate How could he what? Love me? *You* do. Or you did.

Pamela Yes. I can't understand yet. Did he love you?

Kate Yes he did. You have to believe that, or everything was worthless ... none of us have any value at all.

Pamela Why didn't you take him from me? I mean away. To live together.

Kate You had done nothing to deserve that. And I loved you too much to do that to you. So did he.

Pamela Don't patronize me, that's too much.

Kate That's not it at all. What if Robin had been *my* husband?

Pamela I wouldn't have let myself fall in love with him.

Kate Oh Pam ... Does it help you to know we didn't always sleep together?

Pamela I think it makes it worse.

Kate Does it help you to know that he was sometimes a bit jealous of us. I mean of you and me. Of the good times you and I had enjoyed together. The past that we shared.

Pamela I suspected that. Yes. But still, resentment wasn't in his nature.

Kate No. He liked us to be happy.

Pamela He wanted everyone to be happy.

Kate He made you happy, Pam. And he made me happy. And don't imagine there was any sacrificing involved. On anyone's part. We were different aspects of his life. He needed both of us. And he never let either of us down. Not in truth, Pam.

Pamela I suppose I know it wouldn't have been a trivial thing. That wasn't him. I suppose I see he must have really cared for you. Oh God, I feel I've lost you both!

Kate You've lost nothing, truly.

Pamela (*rounding on Kate*) Whatever happened to integrity! To honesty! To conscience! And I haven't heard you say you're sorry!

Kate Because I'm not. Both you and he have been a vital and important part of my life. I regret that right now you are feeling pain. I hate that.

Pamela I feel betrayed. By both of you. The two people who have always mattered most to me.

Kate Nothing that Robin and I had between us was stolen from you, Pam. You meant too much to both of us. You must know that deep down. You had a long happy marriage. Is there anything about it you would have had different in all those years?

Pamela does not answer. She is thoughtful and becomes a bit calmer

But if this is the end of our friendship, well, it will be sad. But don't think differently of Robin. He doesn't deserve that. He couldn't help being the man he was. And if it hurts you so much to think of me sometimes in his arms. Well, you were in his arms when I was sitting by the fire for its warmth.

A pause

I know, being the person you are, that you'll understand — a little — even if you can't accept ... not right now ... that there is a bereavement for me too. (*A pause. Then softly*) All that will remain of us is love.

For the first time, Kate reveals something of her suppressed emotion. She holds her fingers to her eyes. Pamela looks towards her. Looks away. Eventually Kate looks towards Pamela. Tentatively she holds out her hand

Pamela I feel tired. (*She looks at Kate's hand but does not take it. She shakes her head*)

A pause

Kate I need you.

A pause

Pamela I don't know. Give me time. I just don't know.

The two women replace their sunglasses and sit in silence as the Lights fade to Black-out

DOGGIES

CHARACTERS

Thelma (with a Pekinese)
Eleanor (with a Corgi/mongrel)

The dogs are arm-puppets

Scene — a seaside promenade
Time — the present

The esplanade of a seaside resort. A sunny day

*Two empty deckchairs are set c. There is the sound of barking off. Eleanor
and Thelma can be heard calling to their dogs*

Eleanor (*off*) Here, boy! Robbie! Come, Robbie! Heel! Bad dog! Down!
Down!

Thelma (*off*) Come along, sweetie! Come to Mummy, darling! There's a
good little doggie! Oops! Down, pet! Down, darling! Mind Mummy's
skirt!

Eventually Thelma enters

*She is carrying a cream-coloured Pekinese dog, wrapped in a pink towel,
dabbing at the dog's paws as she comes in. Thelma wears a large flat beige
tammy on her head, echoing the colour of her dog, indeed, with its wide head
and ears the dog quite resembles its mistress. Thelma sits on a chair and
towels the dog*

Who's a good doggie, then? Nice walkies? Let's get all that sandy-wandy
off those little paw-paws, shall we?

Eleanor enters with her dog

*She also has her dog in a towel, a dirty one, and the dog is giving her a hard
time. Eleanor wears a high woollen hat with bobble on top. Her dog has
pricked ears and is a rough mutt resembling a Corgi, slightly. Eleanor is also
carrying a small plastic bag. She makes her way across to the side of the stage
and throws away the bag*

Eleanor Robbie! Will you be still! Stop it! Bad dog! Will you give over!

*She makes her way to the other chair and flops into it holding the dog on her
lap. It gives intermittent struggles as she towels it vigorously. The Pekinese
is as good as gold*

Thelma Oh they do so love their romp on the beach, don't they?

Eleanor Oh they do. Robbie, be still!

Thelma Still got a lot of life in him, hasn't he? Maybe you should have
walked him a bit longer.

Eleanor We've been out for two hours, if you must know.

Thelma Oh, sorry.

Eleanor Robbie is just a very energetic dog.

Thelma So we can see.

Eleanor He's fit. Full of zest. I wouldn't have him any other way.

Thelma No, of course not. (*To her dog*) Must keep them fitty-poos. Mustn't we, San-San?

Eleanor I beg pardon?

Thelma I said it's important to keep them fit. I agree.

Eleanor No, what did you say afterwards? San something ...

Thelma Oh I said San-San. That's our name, isn't it, precious?

Eleanor (*laughing*) Heavens above!

Thelma I don't know what's so funny. It's San-San of Naksaki Samoan Moonbeam, actually.

Eleanor Is it a Pekinese?

Thelma Of course it's a Pekinese. A pure-bred Pekinese. And yours?

Eleanor We're a cross. A Corgi. Sort of.

Thelma Yes. Sort of.

Eleanor They certainly loved playing on the beach together, the pair of them.

Thelma Yes. I simply couldn't keep up with them at one point.

Eleanor Best left to enjoy themselves.

Thelma San-San is very good-natured and friendly. (*San-San growls softly*) Now then, sweetiepie. Mummy's treasure. (*San-San nuzzles her face*)

Robbie growls softly

Eleanor Quiet, Robbie! He's a nice little chap.

Thelma He's a she, actually.

Robbie reacts with interest, nosing at San-San

Eleanor Now, Robbie do behave yourself!

Thelma Please do. San-San is a very sensitive little girl.

Eleanor And there was I thinking she was an animal.

Thelma San-San is a very special little creature. (*To her dog*) And San-San is going to be married to a very handsome gentleman next week, aren't you, baby? Yes, next week when she's ... er ... when's she's — (*whispering to Eleanor*) due.

San-San reacts with interest

Yes. He's a Crufts Winner three times running.

Eleanor Well let's hope she catches him, eh Robbie?

Thelma He's sired several champions.

Eleanor And I suppose he's got a name as long as your arm.

Thelma Naturally, that's for the Kennel Club purposes. But one always shortens it for home use.

Eleanor But San-San ... You might as well have called her Harpic. Actually Harpic is quite a good name for a dog. (*To Robbie*) Harpic! Good dog, Harpic!

Robbie reacts, giving her a look

Thelma Really!

Eleanor Well it's a good name to shout. A dog needs a sharp commanding sound. I remember when we lived in Wimbledon we had a dog called Sailor. Now that wasn't a good name to call. Especially over the common. Especially for my husband.

Thelma I can imagine.

Eleanor But Robbie is very suitable for this one. We got him in Scotland, you see. My husband says he's a cross between an elk-hound and a sporran.

Thelma (*not amused*) How amusing. Your husband must have quite a sense of humour.

Eleanor Oh yes. A ready wit.

Robbie bites at himself

Don't do that, Robbie. Yes, we thought we'd get a smaller dog this time.

Thelma Smaller than what?

Eleanor Smaller than a Great Dane.

Thelma Yes. He's certainly smaller than that.

Eleanor I always liked big dogs. The bigger the better. People look at you when you've got a big dog. I had a Great Dane once. Had him for years. I suppose he was living on borrowed time in the end.

Thelma What do you mean?

Eleanor Well, he keeled over and died right there in the park. Right in the middle of his morning walk.

Thelma How terrible!

Eleanor It was. I don't know what I'd have done without my friend Ida. A very resourceful woman, Ida. I was carrying him, you see. A Great Dane is no light weight.

Thelma I can imagine. Especially a dead one.

Eleanor Exactly. I was at my wit's end.

Thelma I can imagine.

Eleanor And we couldn't leave him lying there in the park.

Thelma Oh no! Whatever did you do?

Eleanor Well, Ida went home and got this enormous suitcase.

Thelma What a good idea.

Eleanor But then the suitcase was so dreadfully heavy we could hardly manage. We were completely finished by the time we reached the high road.

Thelma How awful!

Eleanor But then a young man came up and offered to carry our heavy case across the road for us.

Thelma How marvellous!

Eleanor Well — he carried it across the road all right. Then he ran off with it.

Thelma Oh! How awful!

Eleanor Yes. We don't always seem to have a lot of luck with dogs. (*Pause*) I had a Pyrenean. I thought it would be useful to spin its hair and make jumpers and things. But it never seemed to grow all that long. You'd have thought I'd have got a pair of mittens, wouldn't you?

Thelma You'd have thought.

Eleanor I only ever got one.

Thelma What a shame.

Eleanor Had to be an oven-glove.

Thelma Well that's useful.

Eleanor I gave it to my sister.

Thelma The oven-glove?

Eleanor No, the dog. And would you believe it grew masses of hair afterwards. And she knitted herself a cosy travel rug.

Thelma I can see what you mean by bad luck.

Eleanor Yes. So that's why we got Robbie here. He didn't cost us anything. Came from the dog shelter.

Robbie lays his head on Eleanor's shoulders

Thelma Well I hope this one works out.

Robbie gives Thelma a look. He growls

Eleanor Quiet, Robbie.

Robbie growls again

Thelma Have you thought of taking him to obedience classes? I took San-San, although she hardly needed them of course. But I thought she'd enjoy it. Showing all the other dogs how. (*To San-San*) She was instantly teacher's pet, weren't you, darling?

Eleanor As a matter of fact ——

Thelma Most dogs need training classes. San-San loved being with all the other doggie-woggies.

Eleanor We have been, actually. But I'm afraid Robbie treats words of command more in the nature of suggestions. If he likes the idea he obeys. If not — not.

Thelma Where do you go?

Eleanor Mrs Jollyman's on Tuesdays.

Thelma Oh! So do we. Only we go on Wednesdays. That's the day for thoroughbreds. Tuesdays is for mongrels.

Robbie takes a snap at Thelma. San-San growls

Thelma (*to San-San*) It's all right precious. Mummy's not hurt. (*She scowls at Robbie*) Mrs Jollyman is so wonderful with the dogs, don't you think? San-San thinks she's magic.

Eleanor Yes. It's quite sickening the way the dogs do things for her. When she says walk, or sit or heel Robbie behaves as if she's got a sack of doggy-chocs waiting for him. When I try to walk him round with the others he just collapses. And I have to drag him along on his back.

Thelma How embarrassing for you.

Eleanor And it's always your fault, of course. She may be all sweetness to the dogs, but she can be quite waspish with the owners.

Thelma Sometimes, yes. But one does have such confidence in her.

Eleanor The dogs do, that's obvious. "Don't blame the animal!" she booms. She always booms, have you noticed? It's all those complicated instructions. "Lead out of the way! Stand square! Hand over the choke chain! Rotate and down!" I don't understand a word half the time.

Thelma And your dog senses it, of course. That's the point.

Eleanor Last week we were all running in a circle round the hall, perfectly happily for once. Then Robbie stops dead, for no reason whatever. You never saw such a pile-up. I told Mrs Jollyman he's not half as disobedient at home.

Thelma She's used to people saying that, of course.

Eleanor I'm afraid Robbie has a will of his own.

Thelma That's another classic excuse. Any dog can be controlled if it's handled intelligently.

Eleanor You're quoting Mrs Jollyman, that's obvious. I don't think Robbie cares for the spirit of competition in the class. It brings out the worst in him. And I do wish Mrs Jollyman wouldn't keep shouting, "Praise him! Praise him!" so fervently. Makes it sound like a revival meeting.

Robbie bites himself vigorously

Eleanor Don't do that, Robbie.
Thelma San-San is such a little wonder. So clean about the house, aren't you, pet? She knows any number of clever tricks. She can jump over a little stool. And she can play dead. And she can salute for the Queen. And she knows every word I say, don't you, San-San?

San-San nods

Thelma And she's wonderful with children.
Eleanor Have you got children?
Thelma No. Have you?
Eleanor Oh no. You don't need a child if you've got a dog.
Thelma Quite. A dog will keep a marriage together far better than children, I always think.
Eleanor No question. Dogs may grow but they stay the same character. They don't have a personality change. They don't grow up and treat you like dirt.
Thelma You're better off with a dog any day. Isn't that so, San-San? Eh? Yes, if you love them and care for them and treat them well, they'll be your loyal companions for always.

San-San nuzzles Thelma

Eleanor And if they don't you can always get another one.

Robbie gives Eleanor a look

Thelma Some say you're better off with a dog than a husband.
Eleanor I'm inclined to agree.
Thelma They don't grumble the whole evening if you're a few minutes late with the dinner.
Eleanor And they don't argue about which TV programme to watch.
Thelma And if you're delayed at the shops they don't get bad-tempered waiting in the car.
Eleanor They always greet you with an enthusiastic welcome, no matter what.
Thelma Always.

Eleanor They never come home the worse for drink.

Thelma They don't have a mother who checks you've salted the potatoes.

Eleanor A dog can give you all you could wish in the way of undemanding, uncritical lifelong devotion.

Thelma In fact, there's very little a husband can do that a dog can't, is there?

Eleanor Well ... there is one thing ...

Thelma (*after a thought*) Oh yes, of course. Put up shelves.

Eleanor Yes. That as well.

Robbie bites himself yet again

Robbie!

Thelma Have you ever thought of having him clipped?

Eleanor No.

Thelma There's a Poodle Parlour in Rosemary Road. We go there, don't we, San-San? San-San just loves the young lady who attends to her. So looks forward to her shampoo and styling. And she has her little nails cut and polished, don't you, darling? She just loves every minute.

San-San sinks her head down dejectedly

Eleanor It always looks more suited to lap-dogs. Robbie is not a lap-dog. Well I know he's sitting on my knee now ...

Thelma Oh no, I agree. He belongs outdoors in a kennel, I'd say.

Robbie reacts, giving Thelma a look

Eleanor No, he's quite happy under the dresser in the kitchen.

Thelma Heavens, San-San would just hate to live in the kitchen. She has a hand-woven basket with a silk cushion in the sitting-room. It has a simply sweet little Oriental design all over it. Sort of Chinese writing. We've no idea what it says, have we, San-San? But something nice I know. Like, San-San is the best little doggie in the world.

Robbie bites himself obscenely

Eleanor Robbie! Stop that!

Thelma I do think you should have him clipped. Or brushed.

Eleanor He may have a flea.

Thelma Oh no! (*She draws away*)

Eleanor He got them once before. They bred in the Flokati. Have you ever heard of that?

Thelma Certainly not!

Eleanor But I think it's just the sand right now.

Thelma I hope so.

Eleanor Yes. My husband dealt with the fleas very effectively. Would you like to know how?

Thelma I don't think it will be necessary, thank you. With our daily grooming and weekly visit to the beauty parlour we don't think there's any danger of anything so nasty, do we, baby? (*To San-San*) No, we won't have any horrid little beasties jumping about on our San-San's pretty coat, will we? Specially when San-San sleeps on Mummy's bed.

Eleanor I personally think that's quite ridiculous — letting a dog sleep on your bed.

Thelma Well it all depends on the dog, doesn't it. I quite understand in your case.

A frosty pause. The two women stare out front. The dogs do likewise

Thelma (*at last*) This beach isn't what it was.

Eleanor What is?

Thelma The people. Those terrible shops. The litter. I mean they go on and on about a little dog dirt. But I always bring my pooper-scooper. And a plastic bag. I see you had one too.

Eleanor It was a sandwich actually.

Thelma (*severely*) Oh. It is the custom nowadays, you know. However, it's true the beach is covered with much worse things than a little dog dirt. A little dog dirt soon gets washed away by the sea. But those other things float in and out on the tide.

Eleanor Oh well, live and let live.

Thelma I find it highly distasteful especially when San-San picks one up. She thinks they're for playing with.

Eleanor In a way they are, aren't they?

Thelma They're certainly not for leaving about the beach to embarrass everyone.

Eleanor They don't embarrass me.

Thelma It's clear our walks of life have been rather different.

Pause. The two women and their dogs stare in opposite directions

Thelma What's more, I do think people with a certain type of dog should keep it on a lead.

Eleanor What type? Big and ferocious?

Thelma No ...

Eleanor Little and vicious?
Thelma No ...
Eleanor Randy?
Thelma Yes! I mean when you have a dog that mounts everything in sight ...
    including a sandcastle ——
Eleanor Robbie is just simply boisterous.
Thelma Have you considered having him neutered?

Robbie reacts and growls at Thelma

Eleanor What and stop all his fun?
Thelma Fun! I think it's outrageous.
Eleanor But you plan to let San-San have her fling. You just said so.
Thelma That is completely different. San-San will be mated respectably in
    nice quiet surroundings. With a desirable dog of the highest pedigree. It
    will all be entirely acceptable and proper.
Eleanor And you'll pay for the privilege.
Thelma Of course there will be a fee. That is quite normal.
Eleanor Sounds like prostitution to me.
Thelma Really! You don't understand a thing about high-class breeding!
    But then why should you!
Eleanor Thank you very much!
Thelma San-San will have darling little puppies who will be extremely
    valuable. That will more than cover the stud fee.
Eleanor As I said, commercial sex.
Thelma Honestly! You don't know a thing about purity of line. Your
    comprehension of this matter is obviously entirely basic. Just like your
    dog's!
Eleanor That's true. Robbie's not particular. He just goes for it. He's
    fathered any number of jolly little pups of all shapes and sizes.

Robbie's mouth slavers open

Thelma I can imagine.
Eleanor Yes. Very virile is our Robbie. If you get my drift.
Thelma Pardon?
Eleanor So I'm sorry to disappoint you about San-San..
Thelma What do you mean?
Eleanor Your San-San likes a bit of rough, if you ask me.
Thelma What are you talking about?
Eleanor When Robbie and San-San disappeared under the bandstand ——
Thelma Disappeared under the bandstand ...?

Eleanor When you lost sight of them, remember?

Thelma (*weakly*) What — what are you saying?

Eleanor I'm saying Robbie made the most of the opportunity.

Thelma Impossible!

Eleanor I'm saying I think you got your dates wrong.

Thelma But — but I didn't see any sign ——

Eleanor Robbie did.

Thelma Oh my God!

Eleanor Sorry. I think you're going to get a little surprise. How do you fancy a lot of little Pekinorgis?

Thelma Oh heavens! (*Angrily*) San-San!

Eleanor Don't blame the animal, as Mrs Jollyman would say. She was obviously doing what came naturally. And having a ball.

Thelma (*livid*) How could you! You could have stopped them! You did it on purpose! You're a ... an anarchist! I know your type. Can't stand any sort of refinement. Even in a sugar bowl!

Eleanor What?

Thelma No! It all has to be crude and uncultivated. You want to make everything squalid and graceless and repulsive. One look at that hat and I knew you for what you were!

Eleanor I'll have you know ——

Thelma Of course you don't care about breeding! Because you don't have any!

Eleanor Take that back!

Thelma You've no standards! And common with it!

Eleanor And you're stuck up! And stupid! And a snob!

Thelma How dare you!

Eleanor I can't imagine what Robbie saw in your spoiled, half-baked mutt!

Thelma Oh! Don't listen, San-San!

Eleanor I wouldn't give your so-called dog house-room! Mine's worth ten of it!

Thelma Yours! I wouldn't have yours for a fortune!

Eleanor And I wouldn't have yours for a floor-cloth!

Thelma (*rising with a shriek of rage*) Oh! Kill, San-San! Kill!

Thelma and San-San leap at Eleanor and Robbie. Eleanor and Robbie make off round the chairs. The women are yelling at each other as they circle the stage. The noise prompts a clamour of dogs barking off stage

Eleanor Stop it! Stop! What's got into you!

Thelma Rip them to pieces, San-San! Tear their throats out! Massacre them!

Thelma is an avenging angel. Eleanor is seriously scared

In this vein, shouting and screaming, the two women chase round the stage and finally run off

The barking of dogs fades into the distance

The Lights fade to a Black-out

FURNITURE AND PROPERTY LIST

SHOPPERS

On stage: Two deckchairs

Off stage: Shopping bags and carrier-bags containing, variously, woollen dressing-gown, two belts, jotter with a fancy leather cover, large screwdriver, KitKat (**Rosemary**)
Shopping bags and carrier bags containing, variously, wisp of satin and lace (camisole), china statuette, can of air-freshener, W H Smith bag containing map, video cassette, envelopes, Jackie Collins novel (**Angela**)

Personal: **Rosemary**: watch, handbag containing powder compact
Angela: ear-rings, handbag containing personal mirror

EARLY BLIGHT

On stage: Two deckchairs
Rug for **Helen**
Walking stick for **Helen**

Off stage: Knitting bag containing wool, needles, etc. (**June**)

Personal: **Helen**: handbag
June: handbag containing seven airmail letters

DANCERS

On stage: Two deckchairs

Off stage: Shoebags containing shoes (**Betty** and **Wynn**)

Personal: **Betty**: spectacles, handbag containing bag of toffees, mirror
Wynn: handbag

LATE FROST

On stage: Two deckchairs
Beachbag with sun lotion (**Pamela**)
Beachbag (**Kate**)

| *Personal:* | **Pamela**: sunglasses |
| | **Kate**: sunglasses |

DOGGIES

| *On stage:* | Two deckchairs |

| *Off stage:* | Small plastic bag (**Eleanor**) |

| *Personal:* | **Thelma**: Pekinese dog puppet wrapped in pink towel |
| | **Eleanor**: Corgi dog puppet in dirty towel |

LIGHTING PLOT

SHOPPERS

To open: Full stage lighting; bright, sunny effect

Cue 1   **Angela** settles down to read   (Page 9)
       Fade to black-out

EARLY BLIGHT

To open: Full stage lighting; bright, sunny effect

Cue 1/2   **Helen** feels a pain in her chest   (Page 19)
       Slow fade to black-out

DANCERS

To open: Full stage lighting; bright sunny effect

Cue 1/3   **Betty** and **Wynn** stalk off   (Page 31)
       Slow fade to black-out

LATE FROST

To open: Full stage lighting; bright sunny effect

Cue 1/4   **Pamela** and **Kate** replace their sunglasses and sit in silence (Page 41)
       Fade to black-out

DOGGIES

To open: Full stage lighting; bright sunny effect

Cue 1/5   **Thelma** and **Eleanor** run off   (Page 55)
       Fade to black-out

EFFECTS PLOT

During each play, there is the sound of waves breaking on the shore. If the plays are performed together, music from a distant military band can be used to open and close each play, providing a link from one to the other.

DOGGIES

Cue 1   As the play opens   (Page 45)
         Sound of dogs barking, off

Cue 2   **Thelma** and **Eleanor** run around the stage, yelling   (Page 54)
         Sound of dogs barking, off

Cue 3   **Thelma** and **Eleanor** finally run off   (Page 55)
         Barking fades

PRINTED IN GREAT BRITAIN BY
THE LONGDUNN PRESS LTD., BRISTOL.